664·06 (H)

Additives

by Rhoda Nottridge

Wayland

Additives
Vitamins
Fibre
Sugar
Fats
Proteins

Words printed in **bold** can be found in the glossary on page 30.

First published in 1992 by Wayland (Publishers) Ltd.
61 Western Road, Hove, East Sussex, BN3 1JD

British Library Cataloguing in Publication Data
Nottridge, Rhoda
  Additives. – (Food Facts)
  I. Title II. Series
  664.06
  HARDBACK ISBN 0-7502-0394-3
  PAPERBACK ISBN 0-7502-1325-6

Series Editor: Kathryn Smith
Designer: Helen White
Artwork: John Yates
Cartoons: Maureen Jackson

Typesetting by White Design
Printed and bound in Belgium by Casterman S.A.

Contents

Are additives new ?

Since ancient times, people have **preserved** food by adding vinegar, sugar or salt to stop it from going rotten. When people could not get fresh food, they used these stores of preserved food to keep them going through hard times.

BELOW
In the 1800's meat was salted in huge vats to preserve it.

Today, the things we use to preserve foods are called additives.

Additives can be natural, such as salt, or made from **chemicals**. We do not normally use them as a food on their own; they are an

addition, which is why they are called additives.

Apart from preserving food, some additives can make food look, taste or feel different. This is not a new idea. The Romans added natural soda to their vegetables, to make them more colourful. They also tried to make bread that looked white, rather than its natural brown colour.

In the eighteenth century, so many people wanted white bread that bakers added ground-up dried bones, chalk and even poisonous white lead to brown flour, to make the bread look whiter.

This might sound ridiculous to us, but the idea of changing how a food looks, tastes, feels and smells is more popular now than ever before.

5

Food processing

We use more additives today than ever before. This is because around three-quarters of the food we buy is **processed** before we eat it.

We carry out some of this processing ourselves at home. For example, we do not eat potatoes raw; we peel, cook and sometimes even add salt to them first. However, most processing is done before food reaches the shops. There are many ways in which food is processed, such as canning, drying or cooking.

Why is so much of our food processed? One of the main reasons is that the way we live today is very different to the way people lived in the past. Nowadays most people live in large towns or cities, far from the land where food is grown. Few people grow their own food; they buy it from shops. Processing food helps to preserve it, so that it lasts longer in the shops and in our homes. Less food is wasted, because it lasts longer. People also eat food from all over the world, all year round. Processing food by drying and canning means that we can eat food which grows in one country in one season at all times of the year.

BELOW Additives gave this processed mousse artificial strawberry-flavour and colouring.

Investigating Food Processing

You can investigate for yourself how food processing has made it possible for us to eat a greater variety of food all year round.

Next time you go shopping, look carefully at the information on the labels of the food you buy. Where does the food come from? Has it been processed in any way? What is the **sell-by date**? Write down the answers to these questions in a chart like the one below.

How many items on your list have been processed to help them travel and keep fresh longer?

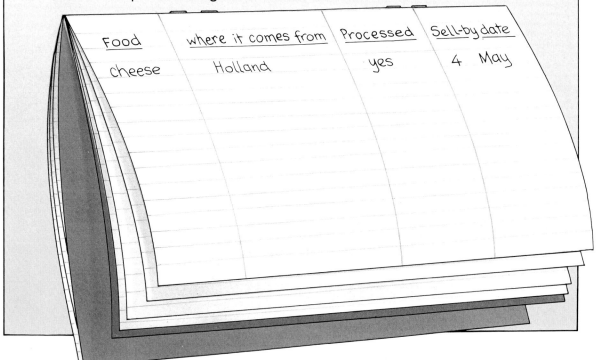

Food	where it comes from	Processed	Sell-by date
Cheese	Holland	yes	4 May

Although processing food helps to preserve it, some of the vitamins and minerals we need to keep our bodies healthy may be destroyed in the process.

New, less healthy ingredients may be added to the product. The more food is processed, the more likely it is that it will contain some of the many different additives.

People who make food are always trying to invent new products which look, taste and feel different, so that more people will want to buy them. These products have sometimes been processed so much that there is little good food value left in them. They often contain too much sugar, **starch** and fat.

Additives are used to give the food **artificial** flavour, colour and taste. With the clever use of additives, something can be made to taste, smell and look like a certain food, without actually containing any of it.

All kinds of additives

Additives which are used today can be divided into groups, depending on what they are used for. In Britain there are twenty-four different types of food additives.

Perhaps the most important types of additives used are *preservatives*, *antioxidants*, *emulsifiers*, *stabilizers*, *flavourings* and *colourings*. They are used to alter the look, feel and taste of food.

Let's look at each of these types of additives in more detail and find out what they do.

Science Corner

You can carry out your own experiment to see how additives are used to change the look, feel and taste of food.

To do this test you will need to make two batches of cake mixture using these recipes. In order to save time, you can make one recipe, while a friend makes the second.

Make sure there is an adult present when you are cooking.

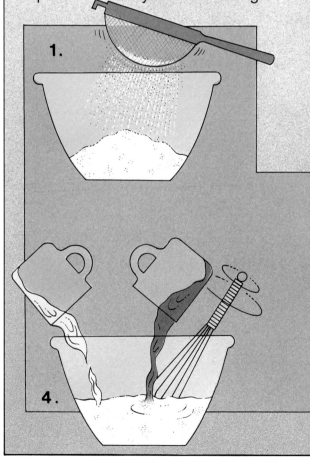

Ingredients for batch 1
(uses additives)

150 g self-raising flour
1/2 teaspoon baking powder
1/2 teaspoon salt
200 g caster sugar
100 g margarine
150 ml milk
1 teaspoon vanilla essence
2 eggs
50 g melted plain chocolate

Ingredients for batch 2
(uses no additives)

150 g plain flour
1/2 teaspoon salt
200 g caster sugar
100 g margarine
150 ml milk
2 eggs

Method
Sift the flour and other dry ingredients into a bowl. Add all the rest of the ingredients, except the eggs and melted chocolate. Beat well for two minutes. Add the eggs and the chocolate (if recipe 1) and beat for one minute. Pour the mixture into a greased, round cake tin and bake in the centre of the oven at 180° C/ 350° F/ Gas mark 4 for about one hour.

What are the differences between the two finished cakes? How has the use of additives altered the look, feel and taste of the cakes?

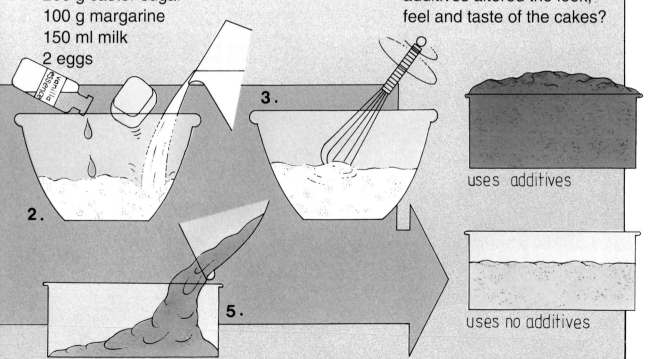

uses additives

uses no additives

Preservatives and antioxidants

ABOVE Preserving fruit by canning or drying will stop it from rotting.

Preservatives are probably the most important additives, because they help us to keep food fresh.

Food rots if it is kept for too long. Adding preservatives helps to stop it from going bad. It prevents poisonous mould or **bacteria** from growing on it. This means that food can be kept in the shops or at home for much longer.

Some preservatives are kinds of **acids**, which are found naturally in some fruits. Vinegar contains a natural acid, which is a useful preservative. It is used to preserve many things, such as sauces, pickles and even some tinned baby food.

Antioxidants

We all need oxygen to be able to breathe. It is a vital part of our lives. However, as well as helping to keep us alive, oxygen also plays an important part in making things **decay**. Without it, the bacteria which causes food to decay cannot work. Oxygen in the air comes into contact with food, which it changes and decays. This is called oxidization.

An antioxidant is an additive which helps stop food decaying by oxidization. If you cut a slice of apple and leave it for a while, it begins to go brown. However, if you squeeze some lemon juice over the slice of apple, it will not go brown. This is because lemon juice contains a natural antioxidant called vitamin c.

Using chemical antioxidants can cause problems. For example, one antioxidant used in potato crisps to stop the oil from going bad can give the disease cancer to rats, if they are fed large amounts of it. On the other hand, small amounts can help to protect rats from getting cancer. It is hard for us to know if our bodies will react in the same way as a rat's body. Antioxidants are only used in food in very small amounts because we are not certain of their effects.

BELOW Which apple slices have been preserved by lemon juice?

Science Corner

You can see for youself how oxygen works on food. For this experiment you will need a pen, paper, an apple and a banana. Leave the apple and banana on a dish for a few days. Each day draw all the changes you can see. The apple will become wrinkled. The banana skin will begin to change colour. What other changes can you see ?

Emulsifiers, stabilizers and thickeners

Some additives help to give processed food a better **texture**. These are called emulsifiers, stabilizers and thickeners.

Oil and water normally separate when they are mixed together. Foods like margarine, salad creams and low-fat spreads are made using both oil and water. Emulsifiers are used to mix together the ingredients, which would normally separate.

Emulsifiers also help to preserve bread longer, and stop tiny bits of fruit in fizzy drinks from sticking together.

Once an emulsifier has been used, a stabilizer is added to stop the mixture from separating again. Thickeners are added to processed food in the same way that we put flour in sauces to thicken them.

Most stabilizers and thickeners come from natural things, but we might not always think they sound very tasty. They include gum from the sap of the acacia tree, wood pulp and seaweed.

BELOW Sap from the acacia tree is used as a thickener. It is drained off from a hole at the base of the tree trunk.

Science Corner

Recipe
This recipe for mayonnaise uses an egg yolk as a natural emulsifier, to bind together ingredients which would not normally mix.

Ingredients
1 egg yolk
1 heaped teaspoon mild
 French mustard
150 ml salad oil
vinegar or lemon juice
salt and pepper

Equipment
teaspoon
measuring jug
basin
hand whisk

Method
1. Put the egg yolk in the basin and add the mustard, salt and pepper.
2. Measure the oil in the jug. 3. Then mix the egg yolk and mustard together with the whisk. 4. Add a drop of oil to the egg and mustard and beat it in well, before adding another drop and doing the same. Be careful not to pour in too much oil at once, as this will stop the mixture from thickening. Continue to add the oil drop by drop, until it is all used up.
5. Stir in the vinegar until the mixture is smooth and all the ingredients are bound together.

Colourings

Colouring food to make it look nicer is not a new idea. In the twelfth century a rare **luxury** called sugar could be found in Alexandria, in North Africa. It was coloured pink or violet. These colourings came from sea snails, an insect and the roots of herbs.

Some of the food colourings we still use today have been additives for many centuries. For example, cochineal is a red colouring which is found in a type of beetle from Central America. Hundreds of years ago, a people called the Aztecs crushed these beetles to use them as a colouring. We still use cochineal as a colouring today.

In the nineteenth century, colourings used in food had become quite dangerous. Colourings which contained poisons such as mercury, lead and copper were commonly used. Governments around the world began to realize they would have to stop the use of certain food colourings, to protect people from eating poisoned food and perhaps dying from it.

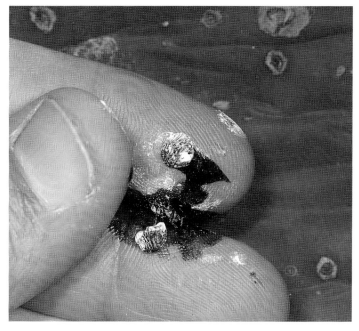

ABOVE
This cochineal beetle has been crushed to show the red dye.

Today there are two kinds of food colourings – natural and artificial. Natural colourings come from plants. For example, beta carotene is the colouring which is found in carrots. Beetroot provides a red colour. The most common single colouring used is caramel. It can be made by over-cooking sugar or using chemicals and is used to colour desserts, soups and many other products.

There is a risk that some people may become ill if they eat foods which contain

certain additives, especially chemical colourings. Children and babies are most at risk, although adults are also affected. Those who are affected may have trouble sleeping, or suffer from rashes, headaches, blurred eyesight and other problems. The **World Health Organization** suggests that to be safe, colourings should not be added to some products, such as baby food.

ABOVE Which of these foods is the odd one out ? It is the sugar, because it contains no colourings.

We expect certain foods to have a particular colour. For example, we would expect bananas to be yellow. However, the colour of food often changes if it is left in strong light or heat. For example, the heat created when food is canned changes the natural colours of both strawberries and garden peas, so that they become brown. Colourings are added to make them look more natural.

A sweet-maker carried out an experiment. A type of sweet was coloured and shaped to look like small copies of real fruit. However, the flavours were jumbled up, so that a sweet which looked like a lemon tasted like an orange, and so on.

Very few of the people given the sweets could guess what flavour they were eating. They expected yellow, banana-shaped sweets to taste of bananas; green, apple-shaped sweets to taste of apples, and so on. This suggests that we connect the taste of a food with a particular colour.

Manufacturers of processed foods also add colourings so that food made on different

Science Corner

You can carry out your own version of the sweet maker's test. For this experiment you will need orange and yellow food colouring and lemon and orange flavouring. You can buy these colourings and flavourings in a supermarket. You will also need some sweet mixture. This is made by whisking together an egg white and 300 g of icing sugar. Divide the mixture into two, adding a few drops of the yellow colouring and the orange flavouring to one half. Add the orange colouring and the lemon flavouring to the other half. Knead each half of the mixture separately, until both pieces are evenly coloured. Divide the two halves of mixture into bite-sized pieces.

Give one yellow and one orange sweet to a friend. Do not tell them what flavour the sweets are. Can they guess correctly the flavour of each sweet? If not, why do you think they guessed incorrectly?

days in different batches will always be a certain colour. Things such as sweets, ice-lollies and drinks are often given colourings because they look pale; adding colours makes them look brighter and more attractive.

There are other ways in which colourings can be used. What a hen eats affects the type of egg it will lay. The eggs from a **free-range chicken** are usually a golden colour, with strong shells. This is because free-range chickens eat a lot of different foods, which they find themselves.

Hens which lay eggs in **battery** farms cannot find their own food because they are kept in cages all the time. The grains they are fed may not contain the natural colours which produce golden yolks.

Egg yolk colours naturally vary from pale yellow to deep orange. But battery hen farmers add red or yellow colourings to the chicken feed in order to control yolk colour. These **pigments** change the colour of the egg yolks, so that they will be the colour that people expect. The rich golden-yellow colour of the eggs we eat is often just an added colouring.

ABOVE Battery farming is considered cruel by many people.

It is often difficult to know whether colourings or pigments have been added to animal feed. In the USA, colourings used by egg farmers have to be stated on the cartons.

The number of artificial and natural colourings used in food is constantly being changed by governments. Many countries allow only certain chemical colourings to be used. This varies around the world. Norway does not allow any artificial colours in food, while Britain allows sixteen and the USA allows seven.

Flavourings and enhancers

Around 3,000 different flavourings are used in food processing today. Like colourings, some flavourings are made using chemicals.

In Britain, a product described as 'blackcurrant flavour' does not have to contain any blackcurrant. It may just contain artificial flavouring, which tastes like blackcurrant. Flavourings are made up of a huge number of things. For example, the artificial flavouring for apple is made up of over 130 different ingredients.

While some additives, such as colourings, may make people ill, flavourings are usually quite safe. Food has to taste good for us to want to eat it. Our tongues will warn us if a taste is bad. So flavourings are usually made from things we would normally eat.

BELOW
Many sweets are artificially flavoured using chemicals.

Science Corner

Recipe with natural flavouring

This tasty recipe for banana milkshake uses only natural flavourings.

Ingredients
1/2 litre of milk
2 or 3 sliced
bananas
(flavouring)

Equipment
large basin
whisk or liquidizer
tablespoon
fork
2 tall glasses

Method
Mash the bananas in the basin using a fork. Add the milk and whisk slowly until the mixture is smooth and frothy. If you are using a liquidizer, place all the ingredients in the machine and turn it on for one minute, or until the mixture is smooth and frothy. Pour the milkshake into two tall glasses, ready to drink.

Flavourings are only used in very tiny amounts. The amount added is often about 1,000 times smaller than the amount of preservative used.

Flavour Enhancers
A flavour enhancer is not a flavouring. It makes the flavour already in food taste stronger.

For many years, Japanese cooks added the water in which they had cooked a type of seaweed to other foods. They found there was a substance in the seaweed which didn't taste of anything on its own, but made other things taste more delicious.

This flavour enhancer, called monosodium glutamate or MSG, is used a lot in Chinese and South-east Asian cookery. Today it is also made from sugar beet and other substances. It is also used in a variety of processed foods, such as packet snacks, soups and flavoured noodles.

The use of MSG has caused some problems. It is possible that extremely large amounts may cause damage to the brains of babies. For this reason, it has been banned from being added to baby food in both the USA and Britain.

It appears that apart from babies, most people can eat a reasonable amount of MSG in their food, without any ill effects.

Some people, however, feel that flavour enhancers spoil our sense of taste; we become so used to stronger flavours that our taste buds become less sensitive.

Sweet solutions

A very large number of processed foods contain sugar. It occurs naturally in some foods. It is also added to many foods, including canned fruit and vegetables, soups, cheeses and sauces. People have become used to added sugar in processed food but now we know that too much sugar is bad for us.

Manufacturers have developed several artificial sweeteners which have the taste of sugar without some of its ill effects. However, we do not know for certain if there are any bad effects from using artificial sweeteners.

ABOVE MSG can be made from wheat too.

Are additives harmful?

However, it is important to remember that allergies and other illnesses are not always caused by the additives in food. Quite a few people are allergic to the actual food itself, such as strawberries, milk or shellfish.

Food for thought

Not all of the effects of additives are known. In New York, USA, an experiment was carried out to see if eating different types of food affected the work of school children. Almost one million children joined in the experiment.

There are two main problems with food additives. The first is that they can be used to hide the true food value of a processed product. The second is that not all of the additives used are good for us. It is thought that as many as one in five additives in use may cause problems for a small number of people.

It has been found that some people are allergic to certain additives. This means that if they eat something which contains the additive, they become ill. It seems that artificial additives are more likely to cause problems.

ABOVE Although these foods contain no additives, some people are allergic to them.

School meals in New York were not very healthy at the time and contained many additives. The experiment involved changing these meals to make them much healthier and free of additives.

When the children ate the new, healthier meals, their results in school tests improved by over 15 per cent. We cannot be sure that this means additives harm the brain. It does mean that wholesome food without additives seems to help children work better at school.

Tests have also been done to see if additives cause other problems for children. Some children who cannot sleep and get angry very easily may find that if they eat food which is wholesome and does not contain additives, they may feel better. It must be remembered that only a small number of children are affected in this way by food additives.

BELOW This meal consists of only fresh food with no additives.

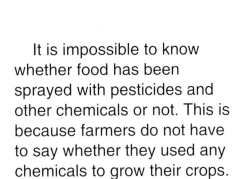

Avoiding additives

There are other reasons, apart from health, for not eating additives. People may want to avoid certain ones because the additives themselves may be made from dairy or animal products which they do not wish to eat. People who follow certain religions, such as Jews, Muslims and Sikhs may be affected in this way.

Pesticide problems

There is a lot of concern about another form of additive, which is used in the early stages of food production, when the food is growing. Pesticides and insecticides are sprayed on almost all fruit, nuts and vegetables when they are growing. They help to keep the growing food free of pests.

However, when we eat food which has been sprayed with chemicals, some of them remain in the food. These can be harmful to our health. Work has been done which shows that there is a small chance of illness for some people who eat large amounts of food that has been sprayed with pesticides while growing.

It is impossible to know whether food has been sprayed with pesticides and other chemicals or not. This is because farmers do not have to say whether they used any chemicals to grow their crops.

People who want to avoid eating foods which may contain chemicals should look out for organically grown fruit, nuts and vegetables. This means that no pesticides, insecticides or other chemicals have been used while the food was growing.

BELOW
Spraying fruit trees to protect the growing fruit from pests.

24

Finding out about additives

If you look on the labels of processed food, you will find a list of the ingredients used to make them. All processed food today must show this information. For example, the label on a packet of biscuits might list sugar, vegetable oil, wholemeal flour and animal fat as the ingredients. If any additives have been used to make the product, these will also be listed here.

Usually, the ingredients are listed in order of the amount used. The amount used is measured by weight. It is very useful to remember this when looking at a label. If, for example, sugar is high on the list on a label for a can of baked beans, we know that a lot of sugar has been added. We may choose to buy a type that contains less sugar. Additives tend to be near the end of the list because they are only used in tiny amounts.

Countries in the **European Communtiy** (EC) agreed that only some additives should be used in food. There are also strict rules saying how much can be used.

ABOVE Take the time to read ingredient labels carefully when choosing which brand to buy.

Those additives which are allowed are numbered and have an 'E' in front of the number. Additives which have E numbers are preservatives, antioxidants, colours, emulsifiers and stabilizers. Food labels must say if flavourings have been used, but they do not have to be named.

RIGHT The law says that food manufacturers must print all ingredients on the label of a product.

If we want to find out which additives have been used in our food, we must be able to recognize their names, so we can check the ingredients label.

Additives must be listed by their group and then their chemical name or number. For example, if a colouring is added, the label must say: 'colouring: sunset yellow' or 'colouring: E110'.

Food manufacturers have a choice of putting either the E number or the whole chemical name on the label. This makes spotting additives more difficult. It means that if a shopper is trying to avoid a certain type of additive, they need to know the number and the name of the additive.

Although E additives are considered safe by the EC, some people have decided it is better to avoid additives and E numbers altogether. The food manufacturers have realized this. They tend to write out the chemical names, rather than an E number on the label which might put off shoppers.

Science Corner

You can investigate for yourself which brands of food contain fewer additives, by comparing labels. You will need a pen, some paper and two different brands of your favourite packet or canned food. Look carefully at the label on each can or packet, noting down on your paper which ingredients each brand contains. Now compare the different brands. Do they contain the same ingredients? Perhaps one will contain less additives than the other, or less sugar. (Remember, the ingredients are listed in order of the amount used.) Which brand do you think is more healthy? Why?

Ingredients: water, potato, carrot, mutton, onion, beef, pearl barley, salt, soya protein (1%) natural gum (guar xanthan), mutton bouillon, sugar, herbs, citric acid.

Ingredients: water, potatoes, carrots, onions, beef, peas, modified cornflour, tomato pure'e, salt, yeast extract, sodium glutamate, spices, herbs colour-caramel.

Making a choice

Many people want to make sure that they do not eat too many additives. Some people want to avoid them altogether. The World Health Organization can tell us the amount of an additive that can be safely eaten by someone each day of their life, without any ill effects. This safe amount is known as the acceptable daily intake, or ADI. When we want to know if eating foods containing certain additives will harm us, we can check the ADI.

BELOW By shopping carefully you can avoid foods which contain a lot of additives.

The use of irradiation may replace additives as a way of preserving some foods. Irradiation helps to slow down the ripening and rotting of food. However, we do not know how safe irradiation is. It may have harmful effects.

If we want to eat less additives, we can cut down on the use of them in our own kitchens. For example, we know that people eat far more salt than their bodies need. We can try not to add salt when we are cooking food and stop using it at the table too.

If we choose foods without additives, it is important to store them properly at home because they will not last as long as food which contains additives such as preservatives.

We have a choice every time we buy food, drinks and snacks. We can decide if we would prefer to buy them with or without additives. By learning to read food labels carefully and by finding out the chemical names of additives, we can choose products we know contain less or no additives.

Careful eating helps us to keep both our bodies, and also our minds fit and healthy.

Glossary

Acids Substances which have a sour or sharp taste.
Artificial Something which does not occur naturally, but is made by people.
Bacteria Very small organisms, which are all around us. Some make living things decay.
Battery hens Chickens which are kept in small cages. They are not free to walk about and find their own food.
Chemicals Substances which, when mixed together, change into something different.
Decay When something rots as a result of chemical changes.
Free-range chickens Chickens which are free to walk around and find their own food.
Luxury Something nice and often expensive, which we do not really need.
Pigments The substances in plants and animals that give them their colour.
Preservatives Chemicals or natural substances which stop or slow down decay.
Preserved To have stopped something from decaying by using preservatives.
Processed When food has been changed, by adding new things and taking some things away.
Sell-by date The date by which time you must eat the food, before it goes off.
Starch A white, flour-like substance found in foods such as potatoes and rice.
Texture The feel of something, for example whether it is rough or smooth.
World Health Organization An organization which is concerned with the health of people all over the world.

Books to read

Food by Terry Jennings (Oxford University Press, 1984)

Food Fun Book by Rosemary Stanton (Hamlyn, 1988)

Health and Food by Dorothy Baldwin (Wayland, 1988)

Healthy Eating by Wayne Jackman (Wayland, 1990)

Food by Kay Davies and Wendy Oldfield (Wayland, 1990)

The Making of Food by Paul Nash (Young Library, 1984)

For teachers

Children's Food by Tim Lobstein (Unwin Hyman, 1988)

E for Additives by Maurice Hanssen (Thorsons, 1987)

Natural and Artificial Additives, Collins Gem series
(Harper Collins, 1991)

Picture Acknowledgements

Ardea 15; Bruce Coleman 13; Chapel Studios *Cover* 6, 11, 19, 22, 23;
J. Greenberg 25, 28; Hulton 4-5; Hutchinson 18, 21, 24; Wayland Picture Library
10, 16; Zefa 26.

Index